The Goddess of Raw Foods

Nwenna Kai

Published by Awaken Media
Pasadena, CA

"Be Your Own Guru"

Published in the United States of America by Awaken Media and Book Surge Publishing

Book Cover Design & Layout - Jamal Talib,The Major Chord Group
Make-up – Megnote Kassa, Kassa Style, Inc.
Jewelry Design - Angelica, Marisposa Creative Design Company
Clothing Design –Runway Boutique, LA, CA
Photographer – Vanessa Vaughn
Food Stylist – Nwenna Kai
Kitchen Design – Euro Cucina, Pasadena, CA

This book is dedicated in loving memory to the life and work of Mohandas K. Gandhi.

THE RAW CONTENTS

ACKNOWLEDGEMENTS

This book is dedicated to a man that changed my life forever, Mohandas K. Gandhi. When I was fourteen years old, I was already having trouble digesting meat and dairy products. I intuitively and psychically felt adverse toward ingesting animals and often would have nightmares after eating meat. On top of all that, I was always one of those very curious children who buried her head in books about Hinduism, religion, diet, vegetarianism, etc and so I found a quote by Gandhi that said,

> "The greatness of a nation and its moral progress can be judged by the way its animals are treated".

And from there on, I decided that I didn't need to eat animals in order to be healthy, to feel full, or to feel normal. Even though the journey has been long, challenging and very lonely since we live in a world where eating meat is a part of the nutritional pyramid and most people often ask me the question of "So what do you eat", I would not have chosen a different path because I know that what I'm doing and practicing is the raw truth.

I am extremely grateful to Gandhi's commitment to being an example of peace, prosperity, and love in so many ways. He was a practitioner of his belief system that has inspired me in the kitchen, in my love life, in my relationships, and in my career. His teachings still permeate the hearts of so many people and I hope that my book will too because its so much more than about raw foods.

My deepest gratitude goes to the global raw foods community for supporting a movement that is transforming people's health and lives, and an entire global consciousness and economy.

Finally, I salute all of you who are taking bold steps in improving your health and the health of your family and community.

The revolution starts at the dinner table!

Prosper All,
Nwenna Kai

IN GRATITUDE

To my faithful, ever-loving, creator, highest cosmic universal Self who is everything and nothing, I am humbly grateful for planting the seed in my heart to serve humankind in such a beautiful and graceful way.

In gratitude to my parents, my sister Zakia, my beautiful and energetic niece Ayanna, Aunt Alana, my host of aunts, uncles, cousins, grandmothers and grandfathers, my business coaches Jamal Talib and Kathryn Mahoney, Women Impacting Public Policy (WIPP) and the Elizabeth Dole Young Entrepreneurial Grant for its financial support, the global raw foods community, Spirit Halima, Brother Jamaal and the Innerlight Radio Family, Blog Talk Radio, Adia May, Dora Jones, Djehuty Ma'at Ra, Billy Locke, Katie Custer, Andre Akil, Megnote, Vanessa Vaughn, Faith Community Church, Agape Spiritual Center, the staff at La Grande Orange Café, my good friend Anita Luckett, Daniel from BookSurge, Paul, Jackie, and Evelyn from Euro Cucina and all of those who have supported and loved me unconditionally, I give thanks.

To the beauty and spirit and the abundance of organic natural living and raw foods. To all the organic farmers and the workers who work the farms, to Whole Foods Markets, the beautiful farmer's markets in the Los Angeles area, to Trader Joes', the mom and pop health food stores, Erewhon in Los Angeles who has long supported raw food vendors, all the raw food restaurants, catering companies, chefs, enthusiasts, websites, internet networks, radio programs, etc... I shout an immeasurably, overflowing, abundant, and an exuberant Thank You, Thank You, Thank You!

MY RAW FOODS STORY
(we all have one)

In my early 20's I was sick and tired of being sick and tired. I had everything: acne, constipation, a thyroid disorder, chronic fatigue syndrome, depression, anxiety, vertigo, sciatica, and a general sense of dis-ease in my mind, body, and spirit. Even though I was eating a mostly cooked vegan diet, I was consuming a lot of processed carbohydrates and meat substitute foods such as processed soy meat, tofu, and tempeh. At the time I was in art school living in a small studio apartment as a graduate student at the School of the Art Institute of Chicago. My constipation was the most debilitating so I figured out one very cold winter morning that if I ate only fresh fruits, salads, juices, and smoothies for a week, that I would definitely go to the bathroom more frequently. So that's what I did. I didn't have any idea that this was the beginning of my raw foods journey.

So for one week, I ate nothing but salads and fresh fruits in the middle of a cold winter in Chicago. And boy, did I go to the bathroom every single day.

Immediately, I had more energy, slept less, and my acne cleared up in a matter of days. So I continued the diet for another week. Slowly my vertigo disappeared and I even felt my depression lift a bit. After a month, I left to go on a yoga retreat and met someone in the salad line at dinner one night. They happened to notice that I was only eating salads. Later I found out that he was a raw foodist as well.

Quickly I was introduced to what it meant to consume a mostly raw foods diet. I went to Karyn's Fresh Corner, a raw foods restaurant and store in Chicago and I took classes, bought equipment, and a lot of books and turned my kitchen into a raw foods laboratory.

After that my life turned into a raw food experiment as I started to learn how to make breads, crackers, spreads, desserts, and nut milks. I learned how to nourish myself so that I would not feel deprived and hungry.

I was astonished at how quickly my health improved in a matter of weeks and months and that was only the beginning.

THE UNEXPECTED AND MAGICAL BIRTH OF MY WORLD-RENOWNED RAW FOODS RESTAURANT TASTE OF THE GODDESS CAFE

In July 2004, exactly a year after I moved from Chicago to the Los Angeles area, I created and founded Taste of the Goddess Café, an organic raw foods vegan café in the Los Angeles area. After working as a segment producer for cable television working long hours, I found myself working all day and coming home at night and making myself food, so I turned my food preparation skills into a business and started catering and delivering food to people. After my producing gig ended, I found a need to expand the raw foods catering business and product line I started on the side in my home kitchen and thus opened up a small café. I didn't know then that it would become what it did, as I did not have any restaurant experience, very little start-up capital, and no idea as to how to run a business. But what I did have was a passion for health and wellness and a burning entrepreneurial fire.

I spotted the coffee shop that became Taste of the Goddess Café while driving along Santa Monica Boulevard in West Hollywood one day just three days after my producing job ended and I just called the broker. To make a long story short, I found myself just three weeks after finding that coffee shop working behind the counter of my own café.

Running a raw foods restaurant is a wonderful experience especially when you know you are not just feeding people, but you are bringing them vibrant health to their lives. It is truly a labor of love.

Even though we closed our doors in November 2007, we continue to spread the message for a healthier, holistic, and prosperous planet and plan to re-open our doors in the near future.

MY RAW FOODS PHILOSOPHY

As a woman, an African American and just a human being, I know the challenges of caring for oneself and it is why I do what I do because I want to teach people how to be healthier in an easy, simple, balanced, and affordable way. There are so many extremists in the raw foods movement and even though it's a great goal to eat a 100% organic raw foods diet, it is not necessary to be truly healthy. Consciousness first and foremost is everything and if I may quote the infamous Dick Gregory when I saw him as a college student at Howard University lecturing about vegetarianism, he said and I am paraphrasing that people who eat "swine" are more enlightened than most vegetarians. I make this point to say that raw foods is a catalyst for better health but it is not the "end all be all" to your health.

I pray that this book serves everyone in a way that resonates with you and your family. I hope all who desire to be healthy take bold effortless steps in creating a healthier environment in your home, at work, and in your communities and make it a habit to do so. Encourage others to do this as well and let that consciousness spread like a virus.

It couldn't be a better time to start taking care of oneself first in order to take care of one's spouse, children, family, community, etc. Learn how to create co-ops, build relationships with your organic farmers and grocers, teach yourself how to grow your own food and thus teach young people in your family and in your community. Encourage yourself to walk to the store instead of drive. Not only do you get your exercise in, but you also save on gas and money, and you help the environment as well. See how abundantly we are blessed when we simplify our lives.

I make self-care a daily practice in my life. I wake every morning with meditation (listening to Spirit) and prayer (talking to Spirit), a morning walk followed by a juice and maybe a salad.

Raw foods is nothing short of a miracle. It not only improved my health, but it provided me with a platform to live my purpose, so I feel blessed each and every time, I go somewhere to speak, do a workshop, or simply share a recipe with someone.

It is so much more than raw foods.

THE ORGANIC RAW VEGAN DIET

The organic raw vegan diet is a simple diet and a surprisingly an even simpler lifestyle once you learn how to integrate it into your life. The organic raw vegan diet is a diet made up of organic, live or raw, unprocessed, uncooked, fruits, vegetables, nuts, seeds, and sprouted grains. We use organic foods because the diet is mainly a detoxifying diet that also properly nourishes and sustains the body, mind, and spirit, therefore eating organically eliminates the unnecessary pesticides and toxins that food contains and thus keeps your body and mind free of toxins. Also foods that come from depleted and toxic soils will thus further deplete and add toxins to the body.

An organic raw vegan diet supplies the body with all the essential vitamins, nutrients, minerals, enzymes, and protein that it needs to thrive and flourish. Most raw foodists have stronger bodies than people who eat a mostly cooked food or meat-based diet. The food is so nutritionally dense because the nourishing vitamins, nutrients, enzymes, and minerals are still intact in the food and they have not been cooked or processed in anyway, thus destroying them.

WHY EAT MORE RAW FOODS?

Eating a mostly raw foods diet will create optimal balance in your life physically, mentally, emotionally, spiritually, and psychologically. Here are just a few of the benefits of a raw foods diet!

Beautiful flawless skin
Naturally muscle toned body
More mental clarity
An abundance of energy
More creativity
Clearer eyes
Better bowel movements
Stronger immunity to the common cold, the flu, headaches, fatigue, etc
A more refined palette
Flexible and stronger bones
Reverses aging
Connects you closer to Spirit
Weight maintenance
Elimination of disease
Better Sex and Better Orgasms
A More Attractive Spirit
An emotionally well-balanced demeanor

A RAW FOODS TESTIMONIAL

Our perception of whole food/raw foods was carrots, broccoli, string beans on a plate. That's it. Our desire was for a healthier lifestyle. But found it was very difficult to eat just that. We didn't want a "get it quick fix scam of a diet". We desired some-thing more. We met Nwenna at a Debbie Allen Event. It was during the holidays. and we had a special dinner party to put together. So we decided to have her come and prepare some food for that special event. ALL were AMAZED! To my surprise we didn't have just raw plain veggie plates. What Nwenna served was a treasure of fla-vor filled LIVE FOOD! The desserts...oh the desserts! Nwenna won all of our hearts that night. Not only did she prepare the LIVE FOOD, she made herself available to our guests to answer questions and share her personal life-changing experience. We all left that night, not only with warm bellies, but a bit more education to take us into the New Year.

From that night, we went to Nwenna's class. What she taught there has been LIFE CHANGING for us! We now eat her "easy to make" recipes on a regular basis. The food is bursting with flavors, easy to make and caters to our very busy schedule. We will continue to go to her classes to discover how we can sustain a healthier
life ... "One Bite At A Time".

Nwenna thank you so much for sharing your gift. We believe that you have added years to our life from it!

What separates you from the rest...your love for life...the love you put in every recipe that you create! We can taste it!

See you on Oprah!

Your Friends,
Derek & Sophia Luke
Actors

BASIC RAW FOODS KITCHEN EQUIPMENT

Eating raw foods can be simple and easy to prepare in a matter of minutes or more elaborate and gourmet according to your palette's desire. You can eat a mostly raw foods diet without any equipment, but you will need to be a little more creative than most.

The Vita-mix Blender - the oven in a raw foodist's world. Even though my clients gasp after I suggest that they invest in this sturdy piece of equipment, they now see the wonderful benefits of such an investment.

Juicer – there are tons of juicer models out there. I've used everything from the Greenstar juicer to the Juiceman Jr. Find a juicer that fits your budget and is easiest to clean so that juicing will seem fun and easy for you and your family. A juicer is used to create lovely and amazing fresh vegetable and fruit juices. It extracts the fiber from the juice leaving you with only the juice to enrich and enhance the life of your cells.

Knife set – a paring knife, a serrated knife, chef's knife and a coconut cleaver for opening up coconuts will suffice. Also having a knife sharpener and block or holder will maintain the lifetime of your knives.

Cutting boards – cutting boards make it easier to slice, dice, and chop all of your raw veggies. A bamboo or wood cutting board adds an organic and eco-sustainable style to your kitchen and lifestyle.

Cake pans – having various sizes for cake pans adds variety to the yummy raw food cakes and pies that you can create.

Storage containers – have ample storage containers on hand to store dressings, cheeses, spreads, ice cream, etc to keep food fresh and thus keep enzymes intact.

Excalibur Dehydrator – ranges in price from $99-$500; used for dehydrating raw foods thus adding texture and warmth to the food.

Teflex sheets – used in your Excalibur Dehydrator to lay food on.

Citrus juicer – used to easily extract the juice from lemons, oranges, and grapefruit. Its great to invest in a very inexpensive citrus juicer as raw food recipes call for a lot of lemon juice.

Spatulas - used to scoop food.

Mesh bags, nut milk bags, cheesecloth – used to make nut milks; purchase unbleached mesh bags that can be washed and reused.

Food processor – a Cuisinart food processor is a top of the line food processor used in most home kitchens; you can find this food processor for as low as $45 but the better ones will of course cost more; this food processor will puree, chop, dice, grind food and more.

Strainers - used to strain nuts, seeds, grains, etc.

Stirring and serving spoons - used to stir sauces, spreads, etc.

Wire beater - used to easily whisk together dressings or sauces.

Saladacco or Spiral Slicer – a spiral slicer can add beautiful textures and artsy shapes to your foods to jazz up your salads, zucchini pastas, etc you can purchase a spiral slicer for $25 or less.

Mandolin – a wonderful chef tool to have in your raw foods kitchen; makes wonderful thin zucchini lasagna slices for your raw foods lasagna and it also is a great alternative in terms of speed and ease for slicing food.

BASIC RAW FOODS KITCHEN STAPLES

DRIED FRUITS
Apples
Cranberries
Figs
Dates
Mangoes
Pineapples
Prunes
Raisins

FROZEN FRUITS
Acai berries
Blackberries
Blueberries
Cherries
Durian
Peaches
Raspberries
Strawberries

DRIED HERBS & SPICES
Basil
Black pepper
Cayenne pepper
Cinnamon, ground
Cumin, ground
Dill weed
Garlic powder
Onion powder
Oregano
Paprika
Pickling Spice

OILS & VINEGARS
Cold-pressed extra-virgin olive oil
Raw apple cider vinegar
Balsamic vinegar
Avocado oil
Walnut oil
Pumpkin seed oil
Coconut Oil

RAW NUTS & SEEDS
Almonds
Cashews
Coconut, shredded dried
Macadamia nuts

Pecans
Pistachios
Pine nuts
Sunflower seeds
Walnuts

SWEETENERS & OTHER SEASONINGS
Raw honey
Maple syrup
Unpasteurized Mellow
White Miso
Agave nectar
Celtic Sea salt
Himalayan sea salt
Braggs Liquid Aminos
Tamari
Nama Shoyu

MISCELLANEOUS
Raw almond butter
Capers
Carob or cocoa powder
Dijon mustard
Nori sheets
Oat groats, whole

Kalamata olives
Sun-dried tomatoes
Vanilla extract
Tamari
Braggs Liquid Aminos
Raw Tahini

SUPERFOODS
Hemp protein
Spirilina
Maca Root
Powdered Green Grass
Food
Cacao
Bee Pollen
E-3 Live
Goji Berries
Juvo

"Nwenna is a walking raw food encyclopedia. She really knows her stuff.
Taking Nwenna's classes has inspired me to not only eat better, but to BE better."

Aliesh D. Pierce, Celebrity Makeup Artist/
Beauty Analyst

HIMALAYAN SEA SALT

A lot of raw foods calls for salt. Many of us have what I call "bad nutrition" programs as the foods that we thought were bad, we really are coming to realize are actually very nourishing to the body.

Himalayan sea salt is the purest salt on the earth and the oldest form of salt. It is also probably the most expensive but these recipes only call for a pinch so it could last you for years if you store it properly.   Himalayan sea salt promotes and supports a healthy libido, it regulates the water content in the body, promotes a health pH level in your cells especially your brain cells, helps to absorb food particles in your intestines thus promoting good digestion, and it reduces the signs of aging.

Himalayan sea salt is mined and washed by hand and therefore contains no environmental pollutants.

3 things could happen when
you eat more raw foods

• You could fall in love with
  food.
• You could fall in love with
  yourself more.
• You could fall in love with
  someone.

Hopefully all three will happen
and you can have a ménage a
trois of the senses.

-Nwenna Kai

Let's Get Started!

The best way to use this book is to use the recipes as a base for your own creative culinary talents. Everyone's palette is different. I like to make spicy and very flavorful food, but my palette actually prefers more bland foods. So honor your palette and your creativity and add more or less garlic if you like.

You can also substitute some items if you find that they are too hard to find or a little too expensive for your budget at the moment. You can substitute agave nectar for honey, but raw honey is sweeter so be mindful. Also some don't consider honey to be vegan because it comes from bees. If you can't find an Asian cucumber, then you can use other types of cucumbers.

We soak nuts to release the enzyme inhibitor to make digestion easier. It also affects the texture and the flavor of the food depending on how long you soak or don't soak. And never use the water from the soaked nuts. It contains the enzyme inhibitors in them. So thoroughly drain the nuts before using them in a recipe.

Befor you approach any recipe, first ask yourself what prep work do I have to do? Is there soaking or sprouting involved? Do I have to marinate anything?

Overall, have fun in the kitchen and don't let raw foods intimidate you!

starters

Breakfast has always been one of my favorite meals of the day. Growing up in Philadelphia, my mother prepared oatmeal very well. She dressed our oatmeal with bananas, brown sugar, and sometimes raisins so what I did with this raw foods version is I added the maple syrup to give it that "comforting down-home feeling". Although maple syrup is not considered to be raw since it is heated in order to be extracted from the sap of a tree, it is full of b-vitamins and it is a good source of zinc and manganese. Since it comes from the sap of the tree and trees have a lot of earth energy, it feeds and nourishes the root chakra that deals with survival and family thus emotionally and metaphysically creating balance and stability in your life.

Now I usually start my day with a fruit smoothie or a vegetable juice, but as a child, oatmeal was always a favorite of mine. It was like comfort food for me.

Even if you decide to cook this recipe, use honey, agave, or maple syrup and add fresh raw fruit and raisins to the mix. It is an excellent food for babies and children as well.

rawsome oatmeal

2 cups fresh oats (soaked
overnight in water)
1 cup raisins
2 tablespoons maple
syrup
½ cup fresh strawber-
ries, blueberries, or black
berries (sliced for gar-
nishing)

½ banana
(sliced for garnishing)
pinch of sea salt

Place the oats, raisins,
maple syrup, and salt
in the Vita-mix blender.
Blend for 30 seconds.

Scoop mixture out of
blender and garnish with
berries and bananas. Add
more maple syrup as de-
sired.

easy apple sauce

4 fuji apples (sliced in
halves)
½ teaspoon cinnamon
½ cup raisins

¼ teaspoon nutmeg
1 teaspoon maple syrup
pinch of sea salt

Blend all ingredients in a
Vita-mix blender for 30
seconds. Leave the mixt-

ture slightly chunky or
if you want it smoother,
blend it longer.

raw breakfast scramble

1 cup finely chopped cauliflower
½ cup chopped red bell pepper
½ cup chopped red onion
½ cup chopped white onion
½ cup chopped cilantro
2 scallions chopped
1 teaspoon tumeric
½ teaspoon nutritional yeast

3 tablespoons olive oil
1 tablespoon Braggs liquid aminos
2 garlic cloves (minced)
1 tablespoon chives (for garnishing and taste)
½ avocado (optional)
pinch of sea salt
pinch of black pepper

Whisk together the olive oil, Braggs, nutritional yeast, tumeric and garlic in one mixing bowl. In another mixing bowl, combine all the other ingredients.
Combine the olive oil mixture with the cauliflower, pepper, and onion mixture until well combined.

Toss the olive oil generously throughout the vegetables. Lay out the mixture onto a dehydrator screen with a Teflex sheet and dehydrate for 2-4 hours.

Garnish with chives.

mushroom sausage

The meaty texture you get from mushrooms is a wonderful substitute if you are craving meat or the texture of meat.

1 cup chopped Portobello mushrooms
1 cup chopped cremini mushrooms
2 cups chopped button mushrooms
1 cup chopped eggplant
1 cup almonds (soaked 8 hours)
½ cup sunflower seeds (soaked 2 hours)
½ cup pumpkin seeds (soaked 8 hours)

4 scallions chopped
3 cloves garlic (minced)
1 tablespoon coriander
1 tablespoon thyme
a few sprigs of fresh rosemary (finely chopped)
3 tablespoons olive oil
3 tablespoons of Braggs liquid aminos
a pinch of sea salt
a pinch of black pepper

Whisk together the Braggs liquid aminos, sea salt, black pepper, olive oil, coriander, thyme, and the rosemary. Toss all the mushrooms and eggplant in the mixture until well marinated for about 20 minutes. In a food processor process the almonds, sunflower seeds, and pumpkin seeds into fine pieces. Do not overprocess.

Then process the mushroom mixture adding the garlic and scallions. Add this mixture to the nut and seed mixture. Stir the mixture until well combined adding salt and pepper according to desired taste. Shape the mixture into flat patties or sausage link shapes and place on dehydrator screens. Dehydrate 8-12 hours.

10 sexiest fruits

the jackfruit
the strawberry
the raspberry
the mango
the pineapple
the kiwi
the cherry
the dragonfruit
the watermelon
the acai berry

smoothies, juice cocktails, & nut milks

"At Taste of the Goddess Cafe, it was a toss-up between the soothing ambiance and the re-freshing, flavorful smoothies as healer."

Yayoi Lena Winfrey
Hapa Writer, Filmmaker, Visual Artist

green goddess smoothie

2 cups spinach, kale, or some type of green leafy vegetable
1 cup frozen mango
2 tablespoons agave nectar
1 pear (seeded)
1 banana
1 cup coconut water

Combine all ingredients in a Vita-mix blender and blend until smooth.

oh so berry smoothie

½ cup almond milk
½ cup strawberries
½ cup blueberries
½ cup raspberries
½ cup blackberries
1 banana

Combine all ingredients in a Vita-mix blender and blend until smooth.

nutty buttery smoothie

We called this smoothie the Monkey Mambo smoothie at Taste of the Goddess Café. It was our best smoothie. We got really creative with it and made it with different milks. It is sweeter with a macadamia milk, but any milk will do. It tastes just like a 'real' milkshake. To make it thicker add more banana or even an avocado. To give it some protein punch, add hemp protein or a few pinches of spirulina. The spirulina will offset the creamy white color but not the taste.

½ cup of your favorite unsweetened nut milk (almond, brazil nut, or macadamia nut milk)
2 tablespoons of almond nut butter

1 frozen banana
2 tablespoons agave nectar
dash of cinnamon
dash of nutmeg

Combine all ingredients in a Vita-mix blender and blend until smooth and thick.

tropical slushy

Juice of 1 Young Thai
coconut
1 cup frozen mango
1 cup frozen papaya
1 cup frozen pineapple
1 frozen banana

1 cup frozen acai berries
(optional: if you can find
frozen acai berries)
1 avocado
1 tablespoon agave
nectar

**Combine all ingredients in a Vita-mix blender and blend
until smooth.**

lemonade cocktail

**This refreshing cocktail was our next best-selling
beverage at Taste of the Goddess Café. It was always made fresh to serve for our guests. And the
ice just makes it feel orgasmic!**

Juice of 1 Young Thai coconut
juice of 3 lemons
1 tablespoon agave nectar
½ cup ice (optional)

**Combine all ingredients in a Vita-mix blender and blend
until frothy.**

citrus party punch

8 blood oranges
1 pink grapefruit
1 cup pomegranates

2 limes (for garnishing)
2 lemons (for garnishing)

Juice oranges, grapefruit, and pomegranates in a juicer.
Garnish with lemon and lime slices. Serve with a punch
spoon in a big punch bowl.

green shaman juice

Every time I do a fast, I make sure I drink at least
64 oz of this juice. After I drink it, I feel like I can
bend spoons and fly off buildings.

4 stalks black kale
4 stalks green kale
4 stalks red kale
2 stalks turnip greens
1 large bunch watercress
1 stalk collard greens
2 cups spinach
8 stalks celery

1 ginger root (as big or
as small as you desire)
juice of 1 lemon
1 apple
1 large bunch parsley
1 large bunch cilantro
2 cucumbers

Juice all ingredients one at a time in a juicer and serve immediately.

durian fruit smoothie

For those of you who are not familiar with durian, you can visit my website at www.the-guide-to-raw-foods.com. I don't like the smell of durian either, but this smoothie will make you dream about durian. Durian is readily available in most Thai markets. If you can't stand the smell of it, it is best to get the frozen durian.

4 whole durian pods or 1 cup peeled frozen durian
meat of 1 Young Thai coconut
juice of 1 Young Thai coconut
2 tablespoons agave nectar

2 frozen bananas
1 whole vanilla bean (chopped finely)
1 cup of your favorite berries (strawberries, blackberries, blueberries)

Blend together in a Vita-mix blender. And enjoy!

"Nwenna Kai was one of the first raw food chefs, on the map, in LA and when I started my raw food experience, I was at her cafe everyday. Her passion and love is clearly in making the healthiest, tastiest food on the planet. Her recipes are great for helping lots of people enjoy the process of losing fat fast and enjoying the taste."

Marcus Patrick
Actor
www.marcuspatrickhotbody.com

nut milks

Making nut milks is easy! You simply choose your nut and combine it with water in a blender. You then strain the pulp through a cheesecloth, mesh bag, or nut milk bag. You need a good green-friendly nut milk bag to make these recipes so that you can use the bag again to make more milk. You can enjoy nuts milks in the morning for breakfast, in a cereal, in a smoothie as a base, or for a dessert. It supplies you with your protein sources. You can also use the pulp to make cookies, breads, pies, and crackers.

brazil nut milk

3 cups brazil nuts (soaked 8 hours)
1 cup water
½ cup tocotrienols
¼ cup agave nectar

Blend the brazil nuts and water in a Vita-mix blender. Then strain the mixture through a nut milk bag. Blend the milk, tocotrienols, and agave nectar in a blender and enjoy!

Tocotrienols are in the vitamin E family and it promotes a healthy heart, flawless skin, and muscle building. They are best used in powder form.

mint cacao almond milk

4 cups almonds (soaked
8 hours)
1 vanilla bean
2 cups water

¼ cup cacao powder
10 fresh mint leaves
¼ cup agave nectar

Blend the almonds and water together and strain the pulp through a nut milk bag to make the milk. Then combine the milk and the rest of the other ingredients together in a Vita-mix blender and serve.

sunflower seed milk

2 cups sunflower seeds (soaked 2 hours)
1 vanilla bean
1 cup water

Blend the sunflower seeds and water in a Vita-mix blender. Strain the mixture through a nut milk bag. Pour the milk mixture back into the blender, add the vanilla bean, blend and serve with or without ice. Save the pulp in a storage container and you can make cookies.

green milk

2 cups hemp seeds
1 cup water
1 vanilla bean
1 cup spinach

Blend the hemp seeds and water. Strain with a nut milk bag. Then blend the milk, vanilla bean, and spinach in the Vita-mix blender until well blended and serve.

macadamia nut milk

2 cups macadamia nuts (soaked 2 hours)
1 cup water
1 tablespoon agave nectar (optional)

Blend the nuts and water together in a Vita-mix blender and strain with a nut milk bag. Serve fresh. You can add agave nectar to it, but the macadamia nuts are already very sweet.

WHERE DO YOU GET YOUR PROTEIN?

If you are raw vegan, vegan, or even vegetarian, if I gave you a dollar every time somebody asked you that question, you'd be a millionaire right? Well here's some of the answers.

almonds
walnuts
pine nuts
sunflower seeds
pumpkin seeds
spirulina (a blue-green algae)
E-3 Live
arame
wakame
avocados
kale
durian
jackfruit
dragonfruit
quinoa
buckwheat
kamut
nutritional yeast

goddess
salad
dressings

balsamic vinaigrette

2 cups olive oil
¼ cup balsamic vinai-
grette
¼ cup sundried tomatoes
(soaked 2 hours)

¼ cup button mush-
rooms (sliced)
2 tbsp. Italian seasoning
4 cloves garlic
1 pinch sea salt

**Blend all ingredients well in a Vita-mix blender. The dress-
ing should be a rosy brown color.**

avocado mango dressing

2 large avocados or 3
small avocados
½ cup frozen mango
4 cloves of garlic

3 stalks scallions
(chopped finely)
2 pinches sea salt
¼ cup olive oil

**Blend all ingredients in a Vita-mix blender until the
mixture is creamy.**

savory sesame miso dressing

1 cup sesame oil
4 cloves garlic

1 tablespoon white miso
1 stalk scallion (chopped)

Blend all ingredients well in blender. You may need to adjust the garlic according to your taste. We used to serve this dressing with our Goddess of the Sea Salad.

cucumber avocado dressing

½ cucumber
2 small avocados or 1 large avocado
juice of ½ lemon

½ cup coconut water
3 cloves garlic
1 tsp. herbamare seasoning

Combine all ingredients in a Vita-mix blender and blend until smooth.

thai lemon vinaigrette

2 cups olive oil
juice of 1 lemon
1 scallion (chopped)
1/8 teaspoon ginger
(minced)

4 cloves garlic
1/2 Thai chiles (chopped
finely)

Blend all ingredients in a Vita-mix blender.

sweet and tangy vinaigrette

2 cups olive oil
1 teaspoon Dijon mustard
1 teaspoon raw honey
1 teaspoon apple cider vinegar

1 fresh mint leaf
pinch of sea salt
dash black pepper

Blend all ingredients in a Vita-mix blender.

This dressing would go well with the apple parsley salad.

spreads, sauces and cheeses

What a difference a spread makes? Having the right spread, nut cheese, or sauce is what makes a main course or entrée delectable. If you can master creating different spreads, you are a raw foods genius. Here are my masterpieces!

raw mayo

½ cup raw pistachios (unsoaked)
½ teaspoon of Paprika
1 cup walnut oil or pumpkin seed oil
Juice of 1 lemon

3 tablespoons raw sesame tahini
2 teaspoons dulse flakes or kelp powder

Blend all ingredients in a Vita-mix blender until creamy.

Dulse flakes and kelp powder are dried forms of seaweed and can be found at your local Whole Foods or any gourmet health food store. You can also purchase them online at various raw food online stores.

'eggless' salad

2 cups cashews (soaked 2 hours)
1 cup raw mayo
1 teaspoon dry mustard
1 teaspoon tumeric
1/4 teaspoon apple cider vinegar
6 garlic cloves
1 cup lemon juice

1/2 teaspoon dried dill weed
2 stalks celery (chopped)
½ cup red onion (chopped)
1/2 cup bell peppers (chopped)
1/2 cup red cabbage (shredded)

Blend all ingredients except the veggies in a Vita-mix blender until creamy. Scoop mixture in a bowl and add the veggies.

pistachio spinach ricotta with dates

4 cups pistachios (unsoaked)
1/8 cup lemon juice
1/8 Braggs liquid aminos
4 garlic cloves

6 Medjool dates (soaked for 1 hour and drained; finely chopped)
2 cups spinach (chopped)
1 roma tomato

Blend all ingredients except for the dates and the spinach in a Vita-mix blender. Once blended until creamy, add the spinach and the chopped dates. Serve on zucchini slices, mushrooms, tomato slices, flax crackers, or

sweet herb cheese

2 cups brazil nut pulp
2 cups brazil nut milk
(unsweetened)
pinch oregano (dried)
1 teaspoon rosemary
(dried)

pinch thyme (dried)
juice from 1 lemon
5 cloves garlic

Blend all ingredients in a Vita-mix blender until creamy.

enchilada cheese

3 cups brazil nuts
(soaked 2 hours)
2 small roma tomatoes
1/8 cup Braggs Liquid
Aminos
3 garlic cloves

1 teaspoon Mexican sea-
soning
½ red bell pepper
(sliced)
water

Blend all ingredients in a Vita-mix blender. Add water as needed.

artichoke spread

8 artichoke hearts (soak for 2 days in water until soft)
½ cup lemon juice

½ teaspoon sea salt
2 cups cold-pressed olive oil
½ teaspoon black pepper

After the artichoke hearts have softened, blend all ingredients in a Vita-mix blender until creamy.

raw mediterranean pate

½ cup raw sesame tahini
juice from two lemons
4 cloves garlic
1 teaspoon pickling spice

1 tablespoon dill powder
1 teaspoon sea salt
1/8 cup olive oil

Blend all ingredients in a Vita-mix blender.

jicama bruschetta

8 plum tomatoes (diced)
½ jicama (shredded)
8 garlic cloves (shredded)
1 cup fresh basil (finely chopped)
1 tablespoon olive oil

pinch of sea salt
pinch of black pepper
pinch of cayenne
1 teaspoon apple cider vinegar

Dice tomatoes. Shred garlic cloves on a shredder. Shred jicama as well. Mix all ingredients in a mixing bowl. Add your basil, sea salt, cayenne black pepper, and apple cider vinegar. Mix well and serve on flax crackers.

pesto sauce

4 cups pine nuts
8 cloves garlic
2 pinches sea salt

2 cups olive oil
4 cups fresh basil

Blend all ingredients except the pine nuts in the Vita-mix blender. Add pine nuts and blend well.

goddess guacamole

3 tomatillos (husked and chopped)
4 large avocados
1/2 red onion (chopped)
1 cup cilantro (finely chopped)
1 plum tomato (diced)

1/8 cup lemon or lime juice
1 garlic clove (minced)
pinch of sea salt
pinch of cayenne
1 tablespoon red chili flakes (optional)

Scoop the avocado meat out of the avocado shells and mash with a fork. Leave slightly chunky. Add the red onions, tomato, garlic, tomatillos, cilantro, lemon or lime juice, sea salt, cayenne, and red chili flakes. If you leave the avocado seed in your guacomole, it will last longer. But guacomole is best eaten when consumed in one day.

I never ate so much guacamole until I started to eat raw. The avocado is a complete food. It is a good antioxidant and it has been used to help people with sexual problems and skin disorders. The brighter the avocado, the more beta-carotene it contains which helps to prevent many forms of cancers. So indulge in your guacamole!

pumpkin seed cheese

4 cups pumpkin seeds
(soaked 2 hours)
1/8 cup Braggs Liquid
Aminos
juice of 1 lemon

4 cloves garlic
2 cups water

Blend all ingredients in a Vita-mix blender until creamy. Make sure there are no chunks in the mixture. If there are, add more water and blend again until creamy.

marinara sauce

8 roma tomatoes
5 garlic cloves
1/4 cup olive oil

5 sundried tomatoes
(soaked 2 hours)
4 tablespoons Italian
seasoning

Blend all ingredients in a Vita-mix blender.

mango salsa

6 roma tomatoes
2 mangoes (peeled, seed-
ed, and chopped)
2 green onions (chopped)
1/2 red onion (chopped)
1/4 cup cilantro
(chopped)

1 small jalapeno pep-
per (seeded and finely
chopped)
1 tablespoon apple cider
vinegar
1 tablespoon lime juice

Combine all ingredients in a mixing bowl and stir. Serve on flax crackers.

raw pine nut sour cream

4 cups pine nuts
(unsoaked)
juice of 1 lemon
3 tablespoons agave
nectar
3 cloves of garlic
1 cup coconut water

2 teaspoons apple cider
vinegar
2 teaspoons herbamare
seasoning

Blend ingredients well in a Vita-mix blender. The lemon juice is very important to the recipe so roll it out to get all of the juice out of the lemon. If it is too thick add some more coconut water to the recipe.

mushroom gravy

1 portobello mushroom
(chopped)
1 cup button mushrooms
(sliced)
1 cup porcini mushrooms
(sliced)
1 tablespoon dried sage
1 tablespoon thyme
1 tablespoon oregano
1 teaspoon tumeric
2 cups raw cashews
(soaked 2 hours)

4 cloves of garlic
1/4 cup olive oil
1 tablespoon nama shoyu
1 celery stalk (chopped)
1 red bell pepper (diced)
pinch of sea salt
pinch of black pepper
water as needed

Blend all ingredients in a Vita-mix blender or a food processor. Add water to your desired consistency and texture. You can sprout brown rice and pour the gravy on top with your favorite vegetables or pour over a portobella mushroom steak.

How to Sprout Brown Rice

Brown rice is considered 'dead' until sprouted. Soak the rice in water for 36-48 hours changing the water twice a day. Then sprout using a sprout jar and cloth for 2-6 days rinsing it twice each day until it is chewy.

unbaked breads and crackers

red pepper flax crackers

2 cups flax seeds
1 cup water
1 red bell pepper
(chopped)
4 tablespoons of chili
flakes

1 teaspoon thympe
1 teaspoon oregano
1 teaspoon rosemary

Mix all ingredients in a mixing bowl. Spread mixture onto a dehydrator sheet onto a screen. Dehydrate for about 12 hours or until crisp on one side and then flip onto the other side.

raisin bread

4 cups brazil nut pulp
(should be wet pulp from
making brazil nut milk)
1 cup flax seed meal
1 cup agave nectar

2 cups raisins
½ cup olive oil
1 tablespoon cinnamon
2 teaspoons sea salt

Combine all ingredients in one big mixing bowl. Hand mix all ingredients thoroughly. Press mixture about ½ inch thick onto a dehydrator sheet and dehydrate overnight. Bread should be a little thick. Store bread in refrigerator.

pizza bread

4 cups sprouted kamut   1/8 cup olive oil
½ cup flax seed meal   4 tablespoons pizza spice

Sprout kamut for 3-4 days. Process sprouted kamut in the food processor until very well broken down. Then add the oil, seasoning, and flax seed meal while still processing the kamut. The kamut dough will turn around in the processor. Allow it to turn until it is well processed. Scoop out the dough and roll until a cutting board with a rolling pin. Add flax seed meal if the dough is too sticky. Roll out the dough and score into a square the size of a dehydrator tray. Lay onto a dehydrator sheet onto a tray and dehydrate for 1-2 hours.

To make flax seed meal, grind the flax seeds in a Vita-mix blender. Make sure the blender is completely dry or you can also use a coffee grinder to grind seeds and muts to make a meal or flour.

tostado shells

4 cups golden flax seed meal
2 cups tomato juice (blend 6 large tomatoes in a Vita-mix blender)
2 tablespoons of Mexican seasoning
1 tablespoon of sea salt

¼ cup garlic oil (Blend 1 cup of olive oil to 4 garlic cloves in a Vita-mix blender)
2 cups cilantro (finely chopped)

Pour all ingredients in a big mixing bowl and thoroughly mix with your hands. Take mixture and lay out on a cutting board. Take a cup or round container and score perfect circular tostado shell shapes. Dehydrate shells for 8-12 hours or overnight depending on humidity and the size of the dehydrator.

herb crepes

4 cups sprouted kamut
2 cups coconut water

2 teaspoons herbamare
1 tablespoon psyllium husk

Blend all ingredients except the psyllium husk in a Vita-mix blender until well blended and watery like milk. Add more water if needed. Stop the blender and add 1 tablespoon of psyllium husk. Blend until it coagulates. Let sit for 3-5 minutes as it becomes more of a gel-like substance. Then spread the mixture onto a dehydrator sheet onto a tray and dehydrate one side for 6-8 hours and then flip to the other side. When finished cut the crepe wrapper into four square crepes.

Kamut is an ancient grain from Egypt and it can be used to make cereals, breads, and crackers. It is a high energy grain rich in magnesium and zinc and it boasts a very high protein level. For many wheat and gluten sensitive people, kamut has been known to be safe to eat.

goddess
salads

Salads are sexy because they are light, easy, effortless, and fun to make and share with a lover. I chose to share with you some of our salads from Taste of the Goddess Café as well as some salads that I love to eat throughout the day.

Salads were my first introduction to the raw foods diet when I was an art school student without a Vita-mix blender and a dehydrator. You can really enjoy the raw foods experience through a salad because you can get really creative with the items you put in it. It is really hard to mess up on a salad, so enjoy making these salads as well as use these salads to create your own creations.

-Nwenna Kai

goddess of the earth salad

2 celery stalks (chopped)
2 cups mixed greens
1 cup spinach
1 cup kale (chopped)
1 cup alfalfa sprouts
1 hothouse cucumber (sliced)
4 carrots (shredded)
1 tablepoon dulse flakes

1 apple (diced)
1 tomato (diced)
1 avocado (sliced)
½ cup cauliflower (chopped)
pinch of sea salt
pinch of black pepper
pinch of cayenne

Combine all ingredients in a bowl and serve with the cucumber avocado dressing.

goddess of eden garden salad

3 carrots (shredded)
1 red bell pepper (sliced)
1 orange bell pepper (sliced)
1 yellow bell pepper (sliced)

2 salsa tomatoes (diced)
½ red onion (sliced)
2 cups mixed greens

Serve with the avocado mango dressing.

apple and parsely salad

2 fuji apples (sliced)
2 granny smith apples (sliced)
½ cup parsley (chopped)
1 avocado (diced)
2 cups mixed greens

½ hothouse cucumber (sliced)
½ cup cherry tomatoes
½ cup raisins
½ cup walnuts (chopped)
1 tablespoon hemp seeds

Serve with one of your favorite Goddess dressings! Your palette will feel so clean and refreshed after eating this salad.

melon summer goddess salad

½ watermelon
1 whole cantaloupe
1 whole melon

½ red onion
olive oil
fresh chives

Dice all the melons and slice the red onions. Drizzle the olive oil on the melons and onions and garnish with fresh chives.

goddess of the sea salad

2 cups mixed greens
1 avocado (sliced)
1 hothouse cucumber
(sliced)
½ cup arame (soaked
and drained)

½ cup wakame (soaked
and drained)
1 tablespoon kelp flakes
1 teaspoon black sesame
seeds
1 cup Wonton noodles
(see recipe)

Mix all ingredients in a mixing bowl. Top with avocado
slices and black sesame seeds. Toss generously with the
savory sesame miso dressing. This salad was our #1 salad
at Taste of the Goddess Café.

*Arame and wakame are two forms of seaweed. You can
find them dried or in powder form at your local Whole
Foods or gourmet health food store, or your favorite
online raw foods store.*

*Seaweed is a powerful source of iodine for the thyroid
glandsand a wonderful source of iron and sodium. It regulates the hormones, enriches the bloodstream, assists in
metabolism, and promotes a youthful skin
color.*

quinoa and fennel salad

2 cups sprouted quinoa
1 small bulb fennel
(shaved)
1 cup cherry tomatoes
1 cup cucumbers
(chopped)
1 bunch of curly endive
(chopped)
½ cup fresh parsley
(finely chopped)
1 cup fresh thyme (finely
chopped)
pinch of Himalayan
sea salt

*Dijon vinaigrette
Dressing:*
1 teaspoon Dijon mus-
tard
3 tablespoons shallots
(minced)
1 tablespoon red wine
vinegar
1/4 cup olive oil
a few pinches of black
pepper
a few pinches of Himala-
yan sea salt

To make the dressing, toss the Dijon mustard, shallots, and vinegar in a mixing bowl and whisk together with   the ol-ive oil, black pepper, and salt. Place all of your veggies in a bowl and generously toss the dressing onto the salad.

This salad is delightful for the palette and it's a cleansing salad as the fresh parsley and fennel awakens the senses of the tongue.

superfood tropical fruit salad

1 cup fresh mangoes (diced)
1 cup fresh papaya (diced)
1 cup fresh pineapple (diced)
1 cup kiwi (sliced)
½ cup pomegranates

¼ cup cacao nibs
¼ cup hemp seeds
Agave nectar
1/8 cup lime juice
pinch of cayenne pepper

Place all ingredients in a large mixing bowl. Pour lime juice over the fruit and lightly sprinkle agave nectar. Garnish with some cayenne pepper and indulge.

dragon fruit and seaweed salad

1/2 cup almonds (chopped)
1/2 cup pumpkin seeds
1/2 cup sunflower seeds
1 fuji apple (chopped)
1/2 cup raisins
1/4 cup black sesame seeds
1 Asian cucumber (sliced)

1 cup arame (soaked and drained)
1 cup wakame (soaked and drained
1/4 cup carrots (grated)
1 large avocado (sliced)
1 cup dried dragon fruit
2 cups mixed greens

Toss with the savory sesame miso dressing or the sweet and tangy vinaigrette.

Dragon fruit is sweet. It boosts the body's immune system, has loads of vitamin C, and is full of fiber.

You can find dried dragon fruit at your local Trader Joe's store. They directly import it from Thailand.

"The expression "TO DIE FOR" hardly expresses the true description of the cuisine at Taste Of the Goddess Cafe but instead "TO KEEP ON LIVING FOR!" is a much better expression! Nwenna Kai is truly one of the 'blessed among' vegans."

-Mother Zitari

Many think soups should be warm and you can make a warm raw soup, but imagine an organic live soup room temperature, so perfect for your throat, your liver, your kidneys, and your blood stream going inside the cells of your body rejuvenating *you*, nourishing *you*, and supplying *you* with everything that your mind, body, and soul desires. This is the magic of a raw foodsoup!
Enjoy!

goddess
soups

seaweed miso soup

4 cups water
1/3 cup white miso
3 green onions (chopped)
2 tbsp dried nori (shred-
ded)
½ cup wakame (soaked
and drained)
½ cup arame (soaked
and drained)
1 tablesoon dulse flakes
½ cup button or shitake
mushrooms (marinated
in garlic oil)

1/2 teaspoon sesame oil
dash of Braggs liquid
aminos
dash of sea salt
dash of cayenne pepper
cilantro (optional for garnishing)
sundried organic black
olives (optional for gar-
nishing)

Pour water, miso, sesame oil, salt, cayenne pepper, and
Braggs in blender and blend for 30 seconds. Pour mixture in a bowl. Add the green onions, button mushrooms,
wakame, arame, nori and the dulse flakes to the bowl and
stir gently. You can blend the mixture longer if you want
your soup base to be warm or you can put your soup in the
dehydrator with all the seaweed and veggies and allow the
mixture to marinate all the flavors. Garnish with olives and
cilantro.

corn and butter nut squash soup

1 cup fresh corn
(shucked)
3 stalks celery (chopped)
2 cups butternut squash
(peeled and diced)
2 green onions (chopped)
1/4 teaspoon nutritional
yeast (optional for taste)

squirt of agave nectar
pinch of sea salt
pinch of paprika
handful alfalfa sprouts
(for garnishing)

Add all the ingredients in a Vita-mix blender. Add water as needed to your desired consistency.

corn chowder

2 cups fresh corn
2 cups pine nuts (un-soaked)
1 tablespoon onion powder

4 garlic cloves
1 stalk green onion (chopped)
handful of alfalfa sprouts (for garnishing)

Blend all ingredients in a Vita-mix blender except for the sprouts. Add water as needed. Garnish with corn and sprouts.

tomato basil soup

6 roma tomatoes
1/8 cup olive oil
1 cup sundried tomatoes (soaked for 4 hours)
1 cup fresh basil (chopped)
2 tablespoons of Italian seasoning

½ cup red peppers (chopped)
6-8 garlic cloves
¼ teaspoon of black pepper
1 teaspoon sea salt

Cut tomatoes in half before blending. Blend all ingredients in a Vita-mix blender until you have a soup-like texture. Add water as needed but not a lot so that it doesn't lose its flavor. Garnish with chopped tomatoes and basil leaf.

RAW FOODS & SEX

Here's the skinny on raw foods and sex. Now I call myself "The Goddess of Raw Foods" so I'm gonna dish it out the best way that I can.

Yes people who eat a mostly raw foods diet enjoy better sex and much better orgasms. Here's why. The more raw foods that you eat, the juicier your body's cells are. So when you have all those organic juices going on, you are unstoppable! Only people who are in great health can truly enjoy better sex and exhilarating toe-curling, bob your head back, hit it on the bedpost orgasms.

A woman who eats a mostly organic raw foods diet will have more "slide to her glide".
A man who eats a mostly organic raw foods diet will have more "pump in his bump".

Not only that, but you feel sexier on the inside and you exude this air of sex and health that can work wonders in and outside of your bedroom.

Of course curling up with another raw foodist is always better, but a vegan or vegetarian will do.

So encourage that *One* to eat *His* or *Her* greens.
I promise you won't be disappointed.

goddess
snacks

goddess granola crunch

2 cup sprouted buck-
wheat
1 cup raisins
1 cup sunflower seeds

3 tablespoons cinnamon
½ teaspoon nutmeg
1/8 cup agave nectar

Hand mix all ingredients together in a big mixing bowl and layer thinly onto dehydrator sheets atop the screens. De-hydrate overnight @ 115 degrees. Eat alone as a snack or serve with sweetened almond or brazil nut milk as a cereal.

Buckwheat is known for lowering the risk of developing high cholesterol and high blood pressure.

buttered asparagus

8 asparagus stalks

Marinate the asparagus stalks in the Savory Sesame Miso dressing for 30 minutes and dehydrate for 1 hour. It makes for a great snack.

protein rich celery sticks

4 stalks celery (cut in halves)
almond butter

Cut 4 stalks of celery sticks in half. Line them with your favorite spread or nut butter. Add hemp protein seeds, spirulina powder, and/or raisins onto the spread or butter. Wrap in a plastic bag and take them to go. You can munch on them in the car.

wonton noodles

meat of 2 Young Thai coconuts
1 teaspoon Braggs liquid aminos
½ teaspoon olive oil

Scrape the meat of two Young Thai coconuts and slice about ½ inch thick the size of linguini noodles. Whisk together the Braggs and olive oil and marinate the coconut meat in a bowl. Place the noodles on a dehydrator screen and dehydrate overnight. Voila! You have wonton noodles to snack on!

zucchini ravioli

This is a great snack or a great party favor to serve up on a platter. They look so pretty on a party platter and people will flock to them because of their zesty flavor and look.

4 green zucchinis
1 cup of the Pistachio creamy ricotta with date spread
1 cup marinara sauce
Dried Italian herbs

Slice 4 green zucchinis and scoop one teaspoon of the Pistachio creamy ricotta date spread onto each sliced zucchini. Place another sliced zucchini atop the spread like a sandwich. Top the sandwich with some marinara sauce and dried Italian herbs. Then dehydrate for 2-3 hours. Serve at a party. Your guests will eat you out of 'house and home'.

my favorite foods

kale, strawberries, blueberries,
blackberries, bananas, avocados,
arame, wakame, dulse, kelp,
Asian cucumbers, Young Thai
coconuts, red peppers, artichokes,
asparagus, mangoes,
jicama, eggplant, celery,
collard greens, zucchini,
pineapples, watermelon, acai berries,
quinoa, portobello mushrooms,
button mushrooms, cauliflower, Medjool dates, spinach, corn,
cashews
and love.

main
courses

"I crave Nwenna Kai's falafel salad and her raw raviolis, forget about it!"

Billy Locke
Wellness Coach,
Health Vision Concepts

raw falafels

3 cups of sprouted chick-
peas (garbanzo beans)
2 cups of sunflower seeds
(soaked 6 hours)
1 red onion
4 large garlic cloves
1 cup parsley
4 tablespoons of lemon
juice

1/2 cup olive oil
1/4 teaspoon cayenne
pepper
2 teaspoons sea salt
2 teaspoons coriander
2 teaspoons cumin
(ground)

Place the chickpeas and the sunflower seeds in a food processor and process until ground but NOT CREAMY! Leave
the mixture chunky. Add mixture to a large mixing bowl.
Then process parsley, onion, and garlic cloves together in
the food processor. Add this mixture to a mixing bowl.
Then add lemon juice, olive oil, cayenne pepper, coriander,
sea salt, and cumin to the mixing bowl. Thoroughly hand
mix or stir all ingredients and make medium sized falafel
balls. Dehydrate balls in a dehydrator on 115 degrees for
8-12 hours depending on humidity.

*You can buy chickpeas that are already sprouted or you can
sprout them yourself. Chickpeas take about 3-5 days to
sprout. Soak the chickpeas for 24-48 hours. Drain water.
Then sprout for 2 days, rinsing them 3 times a day. A 1 1/4
cup of dry chickpeas will yield 3 cups of sprouted chickpeas.*

veggie kebabs and thai almond sauce

You will never want a meat kebab again after making this recipe. This is a great dish to entertain friends and family with at a party!

Veggie Kebabs:
1 green zucchini (diced)
1 white onion (diced)
1 roma tomato (diced)
1 red bell pepper (diced)

1 orange bell pepper (diced)
1 yellow bell pepper (diced)
1 portabella mushroom (diced)

You will need kebab skewers for this recipe. You can purchase bamboo or wood kebab skewers at Sur La Table, Target, or an online culinary store.

Thai Almond Sauce:
1 tablespoon almond butter
1 tablespoon sesame oil

1 teaspoon maple syrup
1 stalk green onion (minced)
1/2 Thai chili (finely chopped)

Whisk together all ingredients in a mixing bowl. Marinate all the veggies in the Thai Almond Sauce and dehydrate for 1-2 hours. Then place veggies on the kebab skewer and serve on a platter.

stuffed portobello mushrooms

2 portobello mushrooms
(de-stemmed)
2 cups Goddess Guaca-
mole
½ cup olive oil

4 garlic cloves
4 sprigs of cilantro

Blend the cilantro, garlic, and olive oil in a Vita-mix blender. Pour mixture onto portobello mushrooms, massage the
mixture into the mushrooms and dehydrate for one hour.
Then take 1 cup of Goddess Guacomole and layer it onto
the portobello mushroom. Garnish with dulse flakes, fresh
scallions, sprouts, or chopped red onions. Great dinner or
snack to have on the go! You can also use another one of
your favorite Goddess spreads, but I love the guacamole.
Eat to your delight!

stuffed bell peppers with your choice of spread

3 Bell peppers (red, orange, yellow)
1 cup of either the mediterranean pate, goddess guacamole, and/or the pumpkin seed cheese.

2 cucumbers
3 tomatoes
3 zucchinis
3 ears of corn
1 cup alfalfa sprouts (for garnishing)

Chop and dice the cucumbers, tomatoes, and zucchinis. Shuck all the ears of corn. Place all the veggies in a mixing bowl. Take 2 tablespoons of your favorite Goddess spead and combine the veggies with the spread. Core out each bell pepper removing the seeds and scoop as much or as little of one of your favorite Goddess spreads in each bell pepper. The mediterranean pate, goddess guacamole, and the pumpkin seed cheese are good choices. Garnish with alfalfa sprouts and eat on the go!

pepper and onion mushroom steaks

4 portobello mushrooms
(de-stemmed)
1 red pepper (diced)
1 orange pepper (diced)
1 yellow pepper (diced)
4 small chippolini onions
(You can use white on-
ions also but chippolini
onions adds a sweeter
taste to the dish)

Marinade:
½ cup balsamic vinegar
1 tablespoon olive oil
2 cloves garlic
pinch of sea salt
pinch of black pepper

Blend the balsamic vinegar, olive oil, garlic, sea salt, and black pepper in a Vita-mix blender.   Marinate the porto-bello mushrooms, peppers, and onions in a mixing bowl with the balsamic vinegar mixture . Dehydrate for 1-2 hours. Top the mushrooms with the peppers and onions and serve.

Portobello mushrooms have more potassium than a ba-nana. Foods that are rich in potassium can reduce the risk of high blood pressure and stroke, but they also balance fluids, and maintain normal heart rhythms.

zesty lasagna

You need a strong palette to enjoy this lasagna. This is not for the faint of the taste buds, so for you Italian food lovers, enjoy!

4 green zucchinis
1 pound spinach (chopped)
4 large tomatoes (thinly sliced)
1 cup marinated button mushrooms (sliced)
3 cups of the Pistachio creamy ricotta date spread
2 cups marinara sauce
½ cup dried Italian herbs

This is how you marinate the mushrooms.
Garlic Oil
1 cup olive oil
4 garlic cloves

Blend the oil and garlic in a Vita-mix blender. Pour mixture generously onto to the sliced button mushrooms and dehydrate for one hour.

On a mandolin, thinly slice the zucchinis lengthwise. Place one layer of the zucchini slices in a lasagna dish. With a large spoon, scoop the creamy ricotta spread onto the zucchini slices. Layer it with spinach, tomatoes, and mushrooms. Layer it with another layer of zucchini slices. Scoop some more of the creamy ricotta spread atop the zucchini and layer it with more spinach, tomatoes, and mushrooms. Repeat this with a third and fourth layer leaving the last layer with zucchini only. Pour the marinara sauce on the top layer and sprinkle the dried Italian herbs on top.

cashew cauliflower mash

1 small head cauliflower (chopped)
4-6 garlic cloves
1 cup cashews (soaked 1 hour and drained)

1/3 cup fresh chives
2 tablespoons olive oil
1 tablespoon nutritional yeast

Process the cashews first in the food processor until smooth. Then add the cauliflower, oil, garlic, and the nutritional yeast and process until very smooth. After processing, place in a bowl and stir in the fresh chives. You can also add the mushroom gravy to the mash if you desire to flavor it up more. Enjoy!

live spinach quiche

Quiche mixture:
4 cups spinach (chopped)
½ red onion (diced)
2 cups button mush-
rooms (sliced)
2 garlic cloves (minced)

½ cup quiche cheese
(see quiche cheese)
few pinches of cayenne
1 teaspoon Braggs liquid
aminos
pinch of sea salt

Marinate the red onions, mushrooms in the Braggs liquid aminos, sea salt and cayenne pepper for 30 minutes in the refrigerator. Add the spinach, red onions, and the mushrooms, to the cheese and stir well. Spread the mixture atop the walnut quiche crust (see recipe).

Quiche cheese:
3 cups cashews (soaked
for 2 hours and drained)
¼ cup nutritional yeast

4 garlic cloves
1 teaspoon sea salt
1 cup water

Place all ingredients except for the water in a Vita-mix blender and blend until well-broken down. Lift the plastic cap of the Vita-mix blender and slowly pour in the water until texture becomes very creamy in texture and whiter in color. Continue blending while pouring the water until mixture is very creamy and smooth. The mixture should have a cheddar taste to it. Immediately store in refrigerator when done.

Quiche crust:
1 cup shredded dried co-
conut

1 cup walnut meal
1 teaspoon coriander

Hand mix all ingredients in a mixing bowl until slightly moist so that it sticks together and press into a pie pan or casserole dish. Add water if you need a little moisture.

hemp burgers

4 cups spinach
6 portobello mushrooms
2 cups sunflower seeds
(ground)

2 cups hemp seeds
½ cup olive oil

De-stem the portobello mushrooms. Place two mush-rooms and a handful of spinach in the food processor and process until fine. Repeat this step with the rest of the spinach and mushrooms. If the mixture is too dry, add 1 teaspoon of olive oil a little bit at a time. Add 2 cups of ground sunflower seed mixture to the same mixing bowl and hand mix thoroughly. Then add the hemp seeds. Form into burger patties and dehydrate for 6-8 hours on 115 degrees or until dry with slight moisture. Serve with one of your favorite Goddess spreads on a napa cabbage leaf or on our pizza bread.

unbaked creamy corn & coconut casserole

Casserole:
4 ears of corn (shucked)
meat from 2 Young Thai
coconuts (diced)
3 chippolini onions
(diced)
3 red bell peppers
(chopped)
3 orange bell peppers
(chopped)
3 yellow bell peppers
(chopped)

Casserole mixture:
1 cup cashews (soaked
1-2 hours and drained)
1 teaspoon nutritional
yeast
1 teaspoon thyme
1 teaspoon tumeric
water as needed

Combine the corn, peppers, onion, and coconut meat and dehydrate for 2-3 hours until very dry.
Blend all the ingredients for the casserole mixture in a Vita-mix blender slowly adding water to the mixture until creamy. Mix the casserole veggies with the casserole mixture and dehydrate again in a casserole dish for 2-3 hours. Garnish with fresh chives.

Nutritional yeast is a complete protein as it contains 18 amino acids. It is a great food for vegans and vegetarians as it contains high levels of B-vitamins and it adds a nutty cheesy flavor to most foods.

red cabbage tacos

1/2 head red cabbage
2 cups goddess guaca-
mole
2 cups mango salsa
½ cup pumpkin seeds

2 cups spinach (chopped)
½ cup green zucchini
(diced)
2 salsa tomatoes (diced)

Separate each cabbage leaf and layer it with guacamole, salsa, spinach, zucchini, tomatoes, and garnish it with pumpkin seeds. Get creative with your taco and add more veggies to it or a different type of seed.

Studies have shown that cabbage has the power to reduce the risk of developing colon cancer because of its high fiber content. It is an excellent source of vitamin C and beta-carotene and a good source of folic acid. When you juice cabbage, it promotes the healing of some ulcers. This vegetable which is low in calories also reduces the absorption of iodine, so if you have a thyroid disorder, watch your intake.

collard green burritos

This is a great raw food treat to take to go. It's easy, inexpensive to make, and you do not need any equipment other than to make the spread with. However, you can just have this wrap with the guacamole and salsa. When I didn't have equipment when I first started my raw foods diet, I ate a zillion of these wraps.

4 collard green wraps (marinate lightly in olive oil)
3 red bell peppers
2 green zucchinis
4 roma tomatoes
2 cups spinach
3 yellow bell peppers

3 orange bell peppers
1 onion
½ cup jicama (shredded)
1 cup Goddess guacamole
1 cup salsa

Chop and dice the veggies to your liking. Choose one of your favorite spreads from this book. The enchilada cheese spread is a great one for this recipe and also the pine nut sour cream and the pumpkin seed cheese recipe. Layer each collard green wrap with your favorite spread. Be generous. Place your veggies in the wrap, add some guacamole and salsa and fold tightly. Enjoy!

zesty nori rolls

4 raw nori sheets
1 cup bean sprouts
1 cup alfalfa sprouts
1 avocado (thinly sliced)

1 cup carrots (shredded)
½ head green cabbage
(shredded)
1 teaspoon dulse flakes

Place all of your veggies in a mixing bowl and generously toss them with the Savory Sesame Miso dressing and the dulse flakes. Then roll your veggies in a nori sheet.

How to Roll a Nori Sheet Without a Sushi Mat

Lay the nori sheet shiny side down on a flat surface. Take your finger and wet it with water. With your wet finger, glide it along the end side of the nori sheet paper. Layer your veggies in the nori sheet paper and then start rolling. The wet side of the nori sheet paper will stick together with the dry side. Then slice your nori sheet at an angle in half and enjoy!

eggplant tomato basil-rich pizza

Eggplant Pizza:
1 eggplant (sliced and marinated in garlic oil)
½ cup fresh basil leaves (sliced)
1 cup button mushrooms (marinated in garlic oil)
2 red bell peppers (chopped)
2 roma tomatoes

Tomato Sauce:
1 cup sundried tomatoes (soaked 1 hour)
1/2 cup sundried tomato water
6 roma tomatoes
1 red bell pepper
1 cup fresh basil leaves
6 garlic cloves
1 teaspoon thyme
1 teaspoon rosemary
1 teaspoon oregano
pinch of sea salt
pinch of black pepper
1/4 cup olive oil
1 teaspoon agave nectar

Blend all ingredients for the tomato sauce in a Vita-mix blender. Marinate the eggplant slices and the mushrooms in garlic oil. Dehydrate for one hour. After dehydrating, place the eggplant slices on a plate and build your pizza. Layer it with the tomato sauce, mushrooms, peppers, and the roma tomatoes. Garnish with the slices of basil leaves.

my top 10 raw food restaurants of all time

1. Taste of the Goddess Café
2. Cilantro Live
3. Au Lac
4. Café Gratitude
5. Karyn's Fresh Corner
6. Arnold's Way
7. Pure Food & Wine
8. Quintessence Cafe
9. Go Raw Cafe
10. Bonobo's Restaurant

-Nwenna Kai

10 sexiest vegetables

the avocado
the asparagus
a hothouse cucumber
broccoli
red cabbage
black kale
portobello mushrooms
the eggplant
the spanish onion
beets

"Nwenna Kai's food is absolutely amazing. Her apple pie is addictive!"

Halima Chancellor
H. Chancellor Promotions

decadent
desserts

apple butter

½ cup raisins (soaked for at least 45 minutes)
½ cup raisin
¼ cup almond butter

1 tablespoon olive oil
1 tablespoon maple syrup
2 dashes cinnamon
1 apple

Process all ingredients in a food processor. The butter should be creamy. You can use as a sweet spread or enjoy as is in a bowl. Garnish with more raisins.

live chocolate mousse

2 cups coconut flesh
12 Medjool dates (seeded and soaked)
3 tablespoons cacao powder

3 tablespoons unsweetened cocoa powder
1/2 cup date water
1 teaspoon agave nectar
a few pinches of sea salt

Blend all ingredients in a Vita-mix blender until the texture is very creamy. Add the date water as needed.

Medjool dates are high in fiber and postassium and are 2% protein.

118

hazel nut kiss frozen dessert

1st Filling:
water from 3 Young Thai coconuts
3 cups cashews (soaked 1 hour)
3 cups coconut flesh

1 teaspoon vanilla flavoring or 1 fresh vanilla bean
¾ cup agave nectar

Blend all ingredients in a Vita-mix blender and pour mixture into a pie pan.

2nd Filling:
3 cups cashews (soaked 1 hour)
3 cups coconut flesh

water from 3 Young Thai coconuts
¾ cup agave nectar
½ cup carob powder

Blend all ingredients in a Vita-mix blender. Pour on top of the 1st filling mixture and allow it to blend together creating a swirling formation. Top the mixture with crushed hazelnuts and freeze overnight. Serve the next day as a frozen pie dessert.

raw chai ice cream

1/2 clove fresh ginger (shaved)
1 teaspoon cinnamon
1 teaspoon nutmeg
2 cups coconut flesh
¾ cup agave nectar
4 cardamom seeds (soak green cardamom pods in a small bowl of water for 5 minutes, take the black seeds out of the green pods, and crush with the back of a spoon)
½ cup – 1 cup brazil nut milk or almond milk (See the chapter on making nut milks)

You need an ice cream maker machine to make this ice cream. Place all ingredients in the Vita-mix blender. Fill the blender with enough brazil nut milk to cover the ingredients. Blend well. Then transfer the mixture to an ice cream maker and process for 60 minutes. After it processes, scoop the mixture into a storage container and freeze overnight.

strawberry ice cream

2 cups of coconut water
4 cups coconut meat
½ cup fresh strawberries
½ cup dried strawberries

¼ cup agave nectar
½ teaspoon of vanilla flavoring

Blend coconut water and coconut flesh first in the Vita-mix blender. Then add the fresh and dried strawberries, agave nectar and vanilla flavoring and blend until smooth. Pour mixture into an ice cream maker for 60 minutes until done. Scoop into a storage container and freeze.

coconut macaroons

6 cups of dried brazil nut pulp (take the pulp from making brazil nut milk and dry in a dehydrator)
¾ cup olive oil
¾ cup agave nectar

½ cup water
1 teaspoon sea salt
a few dashes cinnamon
2 cups dried shredded coconut

Process the nut pulp, olive oil, agave nectar, cinnamon, water, and sea salt in a food processor. In a mixing bowl, place 2 cups of dried shredded coconut in the bowl. Lightly douse the dried coconut with agave nectar. Take an ice scream scoop of the processed macaroon mixture and roll it in the agave coconut mixture forming raw snowballs!

berry carob creme

2 cups coconut flesh
1/2 cup medjool dates (seeded and soaked)
1/4 cup raisins
1 teaspoon cinnamon
1 whole vanilla bean
1/2 cup coconut water

1/4 cup agave nectar
3/4 cup carob powder
1/2 cup fresh berries

Blend all ingredients except the berries in the Vita-mix blender until creamy. Garnish with fresh berries.

banana pudding

As a child, I adored my mother's banana pudding but it always left me feeling bloated. To this day, I still crave the pudding, so I played around with a recipe and we actually served it at Taste of the Goddess Cafe to everyone's delight!

2 cups macadamia nuts (soaked 2 hours and drained)
1 teaspoon vanilla flavoring or 1 vanilla bean
water of 1 Young Thai coconut
3 bananas

meat of 1 Young Thai coconut
¼ cup agave nectar
½ cup walnuts (finely chopped)
½ banana (sliced)

Blend all ingredients except the walnuts and 1/2 banana in a Vita-mix blender until creamy. Garnish with nuts and banana and serve.

RAW FOOD CHEF TIPS AND TRICKS

- Lemon is a natural preservative for food and it makes the fresh food last longer.
- Salt makes food sweet.
- Add avocados to smoothies and it makes them creamier.
- Nutritional yeast is high in protein and b-vitamins and it gives food a "cheddar" taste.
- Soaking nuts for a really long time can take away the flavor of some nuts.
- Flax seed oil gives salad dressings, spreads, etc a nutty buttery flavor and its full of Omega 3 proteins! FUN!
- Psyllium husk is not just a great source for fiber, but in preparing raw foods, it's a great binding agent to help the food bind!
- Date paste is also a great food to use to bind food together.
- To make a flour, grind nuts and seeds in a Vitamix blend. We call it almond meal or almond flour. Use it to make cookies, cakes, and pies.
- If you have had a nut cheese or spread in the refrigerator for too long and you do not want to waste it, spread it onto a dehydrator sheet and dehydrate overnight. Use it as a spice to flavor up your food or crumble it up onto a salad.

"Nwenna Kai is a phenomenal chef. Her in-depth knowledge about food and its' relationship to the body is extraordinary. She is sincerely passionate about cleansing and revitalizing the body. Nwenna is completely driven by her desire to educate people all over the globe on how to eat and live a healthy and balanced life."

Tracie Dean Ponder
producer - ponder this productions, inc.

Nwenna Kai is best known as the creator, founder, and culinary designer of Taste of the Goddess Cafe, an organic raw foods cafe, catering company, and product line in Los Angeles.

She and her restaurant have been featured on E-Entertainment's THS about Diet Fads, Your LATV, LA Magazine, 944 Magazine, The Travel Channel's *Taste of America,* KTLA Channel 5 News with Lawrence Zarian and with Gayle Anderson, H-Monthly, The LA Wave, Innervisions on KPFK 90.7, The Guy Black Show on KJLH 102.3 and Innerlightradio.com.

She was the first recipient for the 2007 Elizabeth Dole Young Entrepreneurial Grant from the organization Women Impacting Public Policy (WIPP) for her work as a health and wellness eco-entrepreneur.

She is a graduate of Howard University in Washington, DC and she received her MFA degree in creative writing from the School of the Art Institute of Chicago.

The Goddess of Raw Foods is her debut self-published book.

She travels the world teaching, lecturing, and sharing her vision for a more healthier, prosperous, and holistic planet.

She divides her time between Pasadena, CA and Philadelphia, PA.

3609854

Made in the USA